MznLnx

Missing Links Exam Preps

Exam Prep for

Elementary Linear Algebra with Applications
Hill, 3rd Edition

The MznLnx Exam Prep is your link from the texbook and lecture to your exams.
The MznLnx Exam Preps are unauthorized and comprehensive reviews of your textbooks.

All material provided by MznLnx and Rico Publications (c) 2010
Textbook publishers and textbook authors do not particpate in or contribute to these reviews.

MznLnx

Rico
Publications

Exam Prep for Elementary Linear Algebra with Applications
3rd Edition
Hill

Publisher: Raymond Houge
Assistant Editor: Michael Rouger
Text and Cover Designer: Lisa Buckner
Marketing Manager: Sara Swagger
Project Manager, Editorial Production: Jerry Emerson
Art Director: Vernon Lowerui

Product Manager: Dave Mason
Editorial Assitant: Rachel Guzmanji
Pedagogy: Debra Long
Cover Image: Jim Reed/Getty Images
Text and Cover Printer: City Printing, Inc.
Compositor: Media Mix, Inc.

(c) 2010 Rico Publications
ALL RIGHTS RESERVED. No part of this work
covered by the copyright may be reproduced or
used in any form or by an means--graphic, electronic,
or mechanical, including photocopying, recording,
taping, Web distribution, information storage, and
retrieval systems, or in any other manner--without the
written permission of the publisher.

For more information about our products, contact us at:
Dave.Mason@RicoPublications.com

For permission to use material from this text or
product, submit a request online to:
Dave.Mason@RicoPublications.com

Printed in the United States
ISBN:

Contents

CHAPTER 1
Introduction to Linear Equations and Matrices   1

CHAPTER 2
Determinants   15

CHAPTER 3
Vector Spaces   17

CHAPTER 4
Linear Transformations, Orthogonal Projections, and Least Squares   25

CHAPTER 5
Eigenvectors and Eigenvalues   31

CHAPTER 6
Further Directions   40

ANSWER KEY   44

TO THE STUDENT

COMPREHENSIVE

The *MznLnx* Exam Prep series is designed to help you pass your exams. Editors at MznLnx review your textbooks and then prepare these practice exams to help you master the textbook material. Unlike study guides, workbooks, and practice tests provided by the texbook publisher and textbook authors, *MznLnx* gives you **all** of the material in each chapter in exam form, not just samples, so you can be sure to nail your exam.

MECHANICAL

The MznLnx Exam Prep series creates exams that will help you learn the subject matter as well as test you on your understanding. Each question is designed to help you master the concept. Just working through the exams, you gain an understanding of the subject--its a simple mechanical process that produces success.

INTEGRATED STUDY GUIDE AND REVIEW

MznLnx is not just a set of exams designed to test you, its also a comprehensive review of the subject content. Each exam question is also a review of the concept, making sure that you will get the answer correct without having to go to other sources of material. You learn as you go! Its the easiest way to pass an exam.

HUMOR

Studying can be tedious and dry. MznLnx's instructional design includes moderate humor within the exam questions on occassion, to break the tedium and revitalize the brain

Chapter 1. Introduction to Linear Equations and Matrices

1. In linear algebra, _____ is an efficient algorithm for solving systems of linear equations, finding the rank of a matrix, and calculating the inverse of an invertible square matrix. _____ is named after German mathematician and scientist Carl Friedrich Gauss.

   Elementary row operations are used to reduce a matrix to row echelon form.

   a. -equivalence
   b. 2-bridge knot
   c. -module
   d. Gaussian elimination

2. The _____ are natural numbers including 0 ' href='/wiki/0_(number)'>0, 1, 2, 3, ...) and their negatives (0, −1, −2, −3, ...). They are numbers that can be written without a fractional or decimal component, and fall within the set {...
   a. Integers
   b. AKS primality test
   c. ADE classification
   d. Abelian P-root group

3. In mathematics, a _____ is a collection of linear equations involving the same set of variables. For example,

$$3x + 2y - z = 1$$
$$2x - 2y + 4z = -2$$
$$-x + \tfrac{1}{2}y - z = 0$$

   is a system of three equations in the three variables x, y, z. A solution to a linear system is an assignment of numbers to the variables such that all the equations are simultaneously satisfied.

   a. -equivalence
   b. -module
   c. Simultaneous equations
   d. System of linear equations

4. In linear algebra, the _____ of a matrix is obtained by changing a matrix in some way.

   Given the matrices A and B, where:

$$A = \begin{bmatrix} 1 & 3 & 2 \\ 2 & 0 & 1 \\ 5 & 2 & 2 \end{bmatrix}, \quad B = \begin{bmatrix} 4 \\ 3 \\ 1 \end{bmatrix}$$

Then, the _____ is written as:

$$(A|B) = \begin{bmatrix} 1 & 3 & 2 & 4 \\ 2 & 0 & 1 & 3 \\ 5 & 2 & 2 & 1 \end{bmatrix}$$

This is useful when solving systems of linear equations or the _____ may also be used to find the inverse of a matrix by combining it with the identity matrix.

Let C be a square 2×2 matrix where $$C = \begin{bmatrix} 1 & 3 \\ -5 & 0 \end{bmatrix}$$

To find the inverse of C we create (C│I) where I is the 2×2 identity matrix.

a. Augmented matrix
b. Euclidean distance matrix
c. Unitary matrix
d. Unistochastic matrix

5. In mathematics, a _____ is a rectangular array of numbers. This way, matrices can record data that depend on multiple parameters. In particular they are used to keep track of the coefficients of multiple linear equations. Matrices are closely connected to linear transformations, which are higher-dimensional analogs of linear functions, i.e., functions of the form f(x) = c Â· x, where c is a constant. This map corresponds to a _____ with one row and column, with entry c. In addition to a number of elementary, entrywise operations such as _____ addition a key notion is _____ multiplication, which displays a number of features not encountered in numbers; for example, products of matrices depend on the order of the factors, unlike products of real numbers, say, where c Â· d = d Â· c for any two numbers c and d.

a. Polynomial expression
b. Commutativity
c. Heap
d. Matrix

6. In its simplest meaning in mathematics and logic, an _____ is an action or procedure which produces a new value from one or more input values. There are two common types of _____s: unary and binary. Unary _____s involve only one value, such as negation and trigonometric functions.

a. ADE classification
b. Operation
c. AKS primality test
d. Abelian P-root group

7. In linear algebra a matrix is in _____ if

    - All nonzero rows are above any rows of all zeroes, and
    - The leading coefficient (also called pivot) of a row is always strictly to the right of the leading coefficient of the row above it.

Some texts add a third condition:

    - The leading coefficient of each nonzero row is one.

A matrix is in reduced _____ if it satisfies the above three conditions, and if, in addition

    - Every leading coefficient is 1 and is the only nonzero entry in its column.

The first non-zero entry in each row is called a pivot.

This matrix is in reduced _____:

$$\begin{bmatrix} 1 & 0 & 0 & 0 & 0 \\ 0 & 1 & 0 & 0 & 0 \\ 0 & 0 & 1 & 0 & 0 \\ 0 & 0 & 0 & 1 & 0 \end{bmatrix}$$

The following matrix is also in _____, but not in reduced row form:

$$\begin{bmatrix} 1 & 9 & 1 & 1 \\ 0 & 1 & 0 & 2 \\ 0 & 0 & 1 & 3 \end{bmatrix}$$

However, this matrix is not in _____, as the leading coefficient of row 3 is not strictly to the right of the leading coefficient of row 2, and the main diagonal is not made up of only ones.

$$\begin{bmatrix} 1 & 2 & 3 & 4 \\ 0 & 3 & 7 & 2 \\ 0 & 2 & 0 & 0 \end{bmatrix}$$

Every non-zero matrix can be reduced to an infinite number of echelon forms (they can all be multiples of each other, for example) via elementary matrix transformations.

   a. 2-bridge knot
   b. Row echelon form
   c. -equivalence
   d. -module

8. A _____ is a symbol that stands for a value that may vary; the term usually occurs in opposition to constant, which is a symbol for a non-varying value, i.e. completely fixed or fixed in the context of use. The concepts of constants and _____s are fundamental to all modern mathematics, science, engineering, and computer programming.

Much of the basic theory for which we use _____s today, such as school geometry and algebra, was developed thousands of years ago, but the use of symbolic formulae and _____s is only several hundreds of years old.

   a. Variable
   b. -equivalence
   c. 2-bridge knot
   d. -module

9. In mathematics, the _____ of a vector space V is the cardinality (i.e. the number of vectors) of a basis of V. It is sometimes called Hamel _____ or algebraic _____ to distinguish it from other types of _____. All bases of a vector space have equal cardinality and so the _____ of a vector space is uniquely defined. The _____ of the vector space V over the field F can be written as $\dim_F(V)$ or as [V : F], read '_____ of V over F'.

   a. Cofactor
   b. Partial trace
   c. Dual basis
   d. Dimension

Chapter 1. Introduction to Linear Equations and Matrices 5

10. In mathematics, particularly linear algebra, a _____ is a matrix with all its entries being zero. Some examples of zero matrices are

$$0_{1,1} = \begin{bmatrix} 0 \end{bmatrix}, \quad 0_{2,2} = \begin{bmatrix} 0 & 0 \\ 0 & 0 \end{bmatrix}, \quad 0_{2,3} = \begin{bmatrix} 0 & 0 & 0 \\ 0 & 0 & 0 \end{bmatrix},$$

The set of m×n matrices with entries in a ring K forms a ring $K_{m,n}$. The _____ $0_{K_{m,n}}$ in $K_{m,n}$ is the matrix with all entries equal to 0_K, where 0_K is the additive identity in K.

  a. Complex Hadamard matrix
  b. Zero matrix
  c. Normal matrix
  d. Regular Hadamard matrix

11. The real component of a quaternion is also called its _____ part.

The term is also sometimes used informally to mean a vector, matrix, tensor, or other usually 'compound' value that is actually reduced to a single component. Thus, for example, the product of a 1×n matrix and an n×1 matrix, which is formally a 1×1 matrix, is often said to be a _____.

  a. Distributivity
  b. Tensor product
  c. Scalar
  d. Self-adjoint

12. In linear algebra, the _____ or unit matrix of size n is the n-by-n square matrix with ones on the main diagonal and zeros elsewhere. It is denoted by I_n, or simply by I if the size is immaterial or can be trivially determined by the context. (In some fields, such as quantum mechanics, the _____ is denoted by a boldface one, 1; otherwise it is identical to I.)
  a. Associativity
  b. Artinian ideal
  c. Orthogonal
  d. Identity matrix

13. In linear algebra, the _____ typically refers to the tensor product of two vectors. The result of applying the _____ to a pair of vectors is a matrix. The name contrasts with the inner product, which takes as input a pair of vectors and produces a scalar.

Chapter 1. Introduction to Linear Equations and Matrices

   a. AKS primality test
   b. ADE classification
   c. Abelian P-root group
   d. Outer product

14. Let S be a set with a binary operation * . If e is an identity element of (S, *) and a * b = e, then a is called a _____ of b and b is called a right inverse of a. If an element x is both a _____ and a right inverse of y, then x is called a two-sided inverse, or simply an inverse, of y.
   a. -module
   b. 2-bridge knot
   c. Left inverse
   d. -equivalence

15. In several fields of mathematics the term _____ is used with different but closely related meanings. They all relate to the notion of mapping the elements of a set to other elements of the same set, i.e., exchanging (or 'permuting') elements of a set.

The general concept of _____ can be defined more formally in different contexts:

In combinatorics, a _____ is usually understood to be a sequence containing each element from a finite set once, and only once.

   a. Rupture field
   b. Near-field
   c. Binary function
   d. Permutation

16. In mathematics, an _____ is a simple matrix which differs from the identity matrix in a minimal way. The elementary matrices generate the general linear group of invertible matrices, and left (respectively, right) multiplication by an _____ represent elementary row operations (respectively, elementary column operations.)

In algebraic K-theory, 'elementary matrices' refers only to the row-addition matrices.

   a. Orthogonalization
   b. Orthonormal basis
   c. Orientation
   d. Elementary matrix

17. In mathematics, in matrix theory, a _____ is a square (0,1)-matrix that has exactly one entry 1 in each row and each column and 0's elsewhere. Each such matrix represents a specific permutation of m elements and, when used to multiply another matrix, can produce that permutation in the rows or columns of the other matrix.

Given a permutation π of m elements,

$$\pi : \{1, \ldots, m\} \to \{1, \ldots, m\}$$

given in two-line form by

$$\begin{pmatrix} 1 & 2 & \cdots & m \\ \pi(1) & \pi(2) & \cdots & \pi(m) \end{pmatrix},$$

its _____ is the m × m matrix P_π whose entries are all 0 except that in row i, the entry π(i) equals 1.

a. Main diagonal
b. Hessenberg matrix
c. Skew-symmetric
d. Permutation matrix

18. In linear algebra, a _____ is a square matrix in which the entries outside the main diagonal (â†") are all zero. The diagonal entries themselves may or may not be zero. Thus, the matrix D = ($d_{i,j}$) with n columns and n rows is diagonal if:

$$d_{i,j} = 0 \text{ if } i \neq j \qquad \forall i, j \in \{1, 2, \ldots, n\}.$$

For example, the following matrix is diagonal:

$$\begin{bmatrix} 1 & 0 & 0 \\ 0 & 4 & 0 \\ 0 & 0 & -3 \end{bmatrix}.$$

The term _____ may sometimes refer to a rectangular _____, which is an m-by-n matrix with only the entries of the form $d_{i,i}$ possibly non-zero; for example,

$$\begin{bmatrix} 1 & 0 & 0 \\ 0 & 4 & 0 \\ 0 & 0 & -3 \\ 0 & 0 & 0 \end{bmatrix}, \text{ or}$$

a. Matrix representation
b. Hessenberg matrix
c. Levinson recursion
d. Diagonal matrix

19. If $A_1, A_2, ..., A_n$ are _____ square matrices over a field, then

$$(A_1 A_2 \cdots A_n)^{-1} = A_n^{-1} A_{n-1}^{-1} \cdots A_1^{-1}.$$

It becomes evident why this is the case if one attempts to find an inverse for the product of the A_is from first principles, that is, that we wish to determine B such that

$$(A_1 A_2 \cdots A_n) B = I$$

where B is the inverse matrix of the product. To remove A_1 from the product, we can then write

$$A_1^{-1}(A_1 A_2 \cdots A_n) B = A_1^{-1} I$$

which would reduce the equation to

$$(A_2 A_3 \cdots A_n) B = A_1^{-1} I.$$

Likewise, then, from

$$A_2^{-1}(A_2 A_3 \cdots A_n) B = A_2^{-1} A_1^{-1} I$$

which simplifies to

$$(A_3 A_4 \cdots A_n) B = A_2^{-1} A_1^{-1} I.$$

If one repeat the process up to A_n, the equation becomes

$$B = A_n^{-1} A_{n-1}^{-1} \cdots A_2^{-1} A_1^{-1} I$$

$$B = A_n^{-1} A_{n-1}^{-1} \cdots A_2^{-1} A_1^{-1}$$

but B is the inverse matrix, i.e. $B = (A_1 A_2 \cdots A_n)^{-1}$ so the property is established.

Chapter 1. Introduction to Linear Equations and Matrices 9

Over the field of real numbers, the set of singular n-by-n matrices, considered as a subset of $R^{n \times n}$, is a null set, i.e., has Lebesgue measure zero.

a. -equivalence
b. -module
c. 2-bridge knot
d. Nonsingular

20. In mathematics, a _____ in a (unital) ring R is an invertible element of R, i.e. an element u such that there is a v in R with

   uv = vu = 1_R, where 1_R is the multiplicative identity element.

That is, u is an invertible element of the multiplicative monoid of R. If $0 \neq 1$ in the ring, then 0 is not a _____.

Unfortunately, the term _____ is also used to refer to the identity element 1_R of the ring, in expressions like ring with a _____ or _____ ring, and also e.g. '_____' matrix.

a. Ascending chain condition on principal ideals
b. Ore condition
c. Unit
d. Ore extension

21. is called _____ matrix or right triangular matrix.

The standard operations on triangular matrices conveniently preserve the triangular form: the sum and product of two _____ matrices is again _____. The inverse of an _____ matrix is also _____, and of course we can multiply an _____ matrix by a constant and it will still be _____.

a. Upper Triangular
b. AKS primality test
c. ADE classification
d. Abelian P-root group

22. In linear algebra, the _____ is a matrix decomposition which writes a matrix as the product of a lower triangular matrix and an upper triangular matrix. The product sometimes includes a permutation matrix as well. This decomposition is used in numerical analysis to solve systems of linear equations or calculate the determinant.
   a. -equivalence
   b. QR decomposition
   c. Crout matrix decomposition
   d. LU decomposition

23. In mathematics, a _____ is a semigroup in which every element is idempotent The lattice of varieties of _____ s was described independently by Birjukov, Fennemore and Gerhard. Semilattices, left-zero _____ s, right-zero _____ s, rectangular _____ s and regular _____ s, specific subclasses of _____ s which lie near the bottom of this lattice, are of particular interest and are briefly described below.
   a. Band
   b. Group extension
   c. Direct product
   d. Formal power series

24. In mathematics, particularly matrix theory, a _____ is a sparse matrix, whose non-zero entries are confined to a diagonal band, comprising the main diagonal and zero or more diagonals on either side.

Formally, an n×n matrix A=($a_{i,j}$) is a _____ if all matrix elements are zero outside a diagonally bordered band whose range is determined by constants k_1 and k_2:

$$a_{i,j} = 0 \quad \text{if} \quad j < i - k_1 \quad \text{or} \quad j > i + k_2; \quad k_1, k_2 \geq 0.$$

The quantities k_1 and k_2 are the left and right half-bandwidth, respectively. The bandwidth of the matrix is $k_1 + k_2 + 1$ (in other words, the smallest number of adjacent diagonals to which the non-zero elements are confined.)

   a. Binary matrix
   b. Skew-symmetric
   c. Modal matrix
   d. Band matrix

25. The set of all symmetry operations considered, on all objects in a set X, can be modeled as a group action g : G × X → X, where the image of g in G and x in X is written as gÂ·x. If, for some g, gÂ·x = y then x and y are said to be symmetrical to each other. For each object x, operations g for which gÂ·x = x form a group, the _____ of the object, a subgroup of G. If the _____ of x is the trivial group then x is said to be asymmetric, otherwise symmetric.

a. 2-bridge knot
b. Symmetry group
c. -equivalence
d. -module

26. In linear algebra, the _____ of a matrix A is another matrix A^T (also written A', A^{tr} or ^tA) created by any one of the following equivalent actions:

- write the rows of A as the columns of A^T
- write the columns of A as the rows of A^T
- reflect A by its main diagonal (which starts from the top left) to obtain A^T

Formally, the _____ of an m × n matrix A with elements A$_{ij}$ is the n × m matrix

$$A^T_{ij} = A_{ji} \text{ for } 1 \leq i \leq n, 1 \leq j \leq m.$$

The _____ of a scalar is the same scalar.

- $\begin{bmatrix} 1 & 2 \end{bmatrix}^T = \begin{bmatrix} 1 \\ 2 \end{bmatrix}.$

- $\begin{bmatrix} 1 & 2 \\ 3 & 4 \end{bmatrix}^T = \begin{bmatrix} 1 & 3 \\ 2 & 4 \end{bmatrix}.$

- $\begin{bmatrix} 1 & 2 \\ 3 & 4 \\ 5 & 6 \end{bmatrix}^T = \begin{bmatrix} 1 & 3 & 5 \\ 2 & 4 & 6 \end{bmatrix}.$

For matrices A, B and scalar c we have the following properties of _____:

1. $\left(\mathbf{A}^T\right)^T = \mathbf{A}$

    Taking the _____ is an involution (self inverse.)

- $(\mathbf{A}+\mathbf{B})^T = \mathbf{A}^T + \mathbf{B}^T$

The _____ respects addition.

- $(AB)^T = B^T A^T$

    Note that the order of the factors reverses. From this one can deduce that a square matrix A is invertible if and only if A^T is invertible, and in this case we have $(A^{-1})^T = (A^T)^{-1}$. It is relatively easy to extend this result to the general case of multiple matrices, where we find that $(ABC...XYZ)^T = Z^T Y^T X^T ... C^T B^T A^T$.

- $(cA)^T = cA^T$

    The _____ of a scalar is the same scalar. Together with (2), this states that the _____ is a linear map from the space of m × n matrices to the space of all n × m matrices.

- $\det(A^T) = \det(A)$

    The determinant of a square matrix is the same as that of its _____.

- The dot product of two column vectors a and b can be computed as

    $$\mathbf{a} \cdot \mathbf{b} = \mathbf{a}^T \mathbf{b},$$

    which is written as $a_i b^i$ in Einstein notation.
- If A has only real entries, then $A^T A$ is a positive-semidefinite matrix.
- $(A^T)^{-1} = (A^{-1})^T$

    The _____ of an invertible matrix is also invertible, and its inverse is the _____ of the inverse of the original matrix.

- If A is a square matrix, then its eigenvalues are equal to the eigenvalues of its _____.

A square matrix whose _____ is equal to itself is called a symmetric matrix; that is, A is symmetric if

$$A^T = A.$$

A square matrix whose _____ is also its inverse is called an orthogonal matrix; that is, G is orthogonal if

$$GG^T = G^T G = I_n,$$ the identity matrix, i.e. $G^T = G^{-1}$.

A square matrix whose _____ is equal to its negative is called skew-symmetric matrix; that is, A is skew-symmetric if

$$A^T = -A.$$

The conjugate _____ of the complex matrix A, written as A*, is obtained by taking the _____ of A and the complex conjugate of each entry:

$$A^* = (\overline{A})^T = \overline{(A^T)}.$$

If f: V→W is a linear map between vector spaces V and W with nondegenerate bilinear forms, we define the _____ of f to be the linear map ^tf : W→V, determined by

$$B_V(v, {}^tf(w)) = B_W(f(v), w) \quad \forall\ v \in V, w \in W.$$

Here, B_V and B_W are the bilinear forms on V and W respectively. The matrix of the _____ of a map is the transposed matrix only if the bases are orthonormal with respect to their bilinear forms.

Over a complex vector space, one often works with sesquilinear forms instead of bilinear (conjugate-linear in one argument.)

- a. Drazin inverse
- b. Tridiagonal matrix
- c. Transpose
- d. Levinson recursion

27. In linear algebra, a _____ is a square matrix, A, that is equal to its transpose

$$A = A^T.$$

The entries of a _____ are symmetric with respect to the main diagonal (top left to bottom right.) So if the entries are written as A = (a_{ij}), then

$$a_{ij} = a_{ji}$$

for all indices i and j. The following 3×3 matrix is symmetric:

$$\begin{bmatrix} 1 & 2 & 3 \\ 2 & 4 & -5 \\ 3 & -5 & 6 \end{bmatrix}.$$

A matrix is called skew-symmetric or antisymmetric if its transpose is the same as its negative.

a. Butson-type
b. Zero matrix
c. Stieltjes matrix
d. Symmetric matrix

28. In the case of Gaussian elimination, it is best to choose a pivot element with large absolute value. This improves the numerical stability. In _____, the algorithm considers all entries in the column of the matrix that is currently being considered, picks the entry with largest absolute value, and finally swaps rows such that this entry is the pivot in question.

a. 2-bridge knot
b. -module
c. -equivalence
d. Partial pivoting

Chapter 2. Determinants   15

1. In linear algebra, the _____ describes a particular construction that is useful for calculating both the determinant and inverse of square matrices. Specifically the _____ of the (i, j) entry of a matrix, also known as the (i, j) _____ of that matrix, is the signed minor of that entry.

Finding the minors of a matrix A is a multi-step process:

1. Choose an entry a_{ij} from the matrix.
2. Cross out the entries that lie in the corresponding row i and column j.
3. Rewrite the matrix without the marked entries.
4. Obtain the determinant M_{ij} of this new matrix.

M_{ij} is termed the minor for entry a_{ij}.

If i + j is an even number, the _____ C_{ij} of a_{ij} coincides with its minor:

$$C_{ij} = M_{ij}.$$

Otherwise, it is equal to the additive inverse of its minor:

$$C_{ij} = -M_{ij}.$$

If A is a square matrix, then the minor of its entry a_{ij}, also known as the i,j, or (i,j), or (i,j)[th] minor of A, is denoted by M_{ij} and is defined to be the determinant of the submatrix obtained by removing from A its i-th row and j-th column.

   a. Cofactor
   b. Complex structure
   c. Coefficient matrix
   d. Resolvent set

2. In linear algebra, a _____ of a matrix A is the determinant of some smaller square matrix, cut down from A by removing one or more of its rows or columns. _____s obtained by removing just one row and one column from square matrices (first _____s) are required for calculating matrix cofactors, which in turn are useful for computing both the determinant and inverse of square matrices.
   a. Minor
   b. Supergroup
   c. Rng
   d. Purification

Chapter 2. Determinants

3. In mathematics, an _____ of a product of sums expresses it as a sum of products by using the fact that multiplication distributes over addition. _____s of polynomials are obtained by multiplying together their factors, which results in a sum of terms with variables raised to different degrees.

To multiply two factors, each term of the first factor must be multiplied by each term of the other factor.

   a. Ordered vector space
   b. Equipotential surfaces
   c. Analytic subgroup
   d. Expansion

4. In vector calculus, the _____ is shorthand for either the _____ matrix or its determinant, the _____ determinant.

In algebraic geometry the _____ of a curve means the _____ variety: a group variety associated to the curve, in which the curve can be embedded.

These concepts are all named after the mathematician Carl Gustav Jacob Jacobi.

   a. Jacobian
   b. Laplace operator
   c. Critical point
   d. Hessian matrix

5. In mathematics, the _____ is a binary operation on two vectors in a three-dimensional Euclidean space that results in another vector which is perpendicular to the plane containing the two input vectors. The algebra defined by the _____ is neither commutative nor associative. It contrasts with the dot product which produces a scalar result.
   a. Differential graded algebra
   b. Row space
   c. Cross product
   d. Formal power series

Chapter 3. Vector Spaces

1. In mathematics, particularly linear algebra, a _____ is a matrix with all its entries being zero. Some examples of zero matrices are

$$0_{1,1} = \begin{bmatrix} 0 \end{bmatrix}, \quad 0_{2,2} = \begin{bmatrix} 0 & 0 \\ 0 & 0 \end{bmatrix}, \quad 0_{2,3} = \begin{bmatrix} 0 & 0 & 0 \\ 0 & 0 & 0 \end{bmatrix},$$

The set of m×n matrices with entries in a ring K forms a ring $K_{m,n}$. The _____ $0_{K_{m,n}}$ in $K_{m,n}$ is the matrix with all entries equal to 0_K, where 0_K is the additive identity in K.

   a. Regular Hadamard matrix
   b. Complex Hadamard matrix
   c. Zero matrix
   d. Normal matrix

2. In mathematics, a _____ is a rectangular array of numbers. This way, matrices can record data that depend on multiple parameters. In particular they are used to keep track of the coefficients of multiple linear equations. Matrices are closely connected to linear transformations, which are higher-dimensional analogs of linear functions, i.e., functions of the form f(x) = c Â· x, where c is a constant. This map corresponds to a _____ with one row and column, with entry c. In addition to a number of elementary, entrywise operations such as _____ addition a key notion is _____ multiplication, which displays a number of features not encountered in numbers; for example, products of matrices depend on the order of the factors, unlike products of real numbers, say, where c Â· d = d Â· c for any two numbers c and d.
   a. Commutativity
   b. Matrix
   c. Heap
   d. Polynomial expression

3. The real component of a quaternion is also called its _____ part.

The term is also sometimes used informally to mean a vector, matrix, tensor, or other usually 'compound' value that is actually reduced to a single component. Thus, for example, the product of a 1×n matrix and an n×1 matrix, which is formally a 1×1 matrix, is often said to be a _____.

   a. Distributivity
   b. Scalar
   c. Self-adjoint
   d. Tensor product

4. In mathematics, _____ is one of the basic operations defining a vector space in linear algebra Note that _____ is different from scalar product which is an inner product between two vectors.

Chapter 3. Vector Spaces

More specifically, if K is a field and V is a vector space over K, then _____ is a function from K × V to V. The result of applying this function to c in K and v in V is denoted cv.

 a. K-frame
 b. Matrix pencil
 c. Symplectic vector space
 d. Scalar multiplication

5. In linear algebra, a _____ is a set of vectors that, in a linear combination, can represent every vector in a given vector space or free module, and such that no element of the set can be represented as a linear combination of the others. In other words, a _____ is a linearly independent spanning set.
 a. Supergroup
 b. Minor
 c. Chirality
 d. Basis

6. In abstract algebra, the _____ of a module is a measure of the module's 'size'. It is defined as the _____ of the longest ascending chain of submodules and is a generalization of the concept of dimension for vector spaces. The modules with finite _____ share many important properties with finite-dimensional vector spaces.
 a. Length
 b. Finitely generated module
 c. Supermodule
 d. Morita equivalence

7. In linear algebra, a family of vectors is _____ if none of them can be written as a linear combination of finitely many other vectors in the collection. A family of vectors which is not _____ is called linearly dependent. For instance, in the three-dimensional real vector space $\mathbb{R}^3$ we have the following example.
 a. Grothendieck group
 b. Derivative algebra
 c. Composition ring
 d. Linearly independent

8. In linear algebra, functional analysis and related areas of mathematics, a _____ is a function that assigns a strictly positive length or size to all vectors in a vector space, other than the zero vector. A seminorm (or pseudonorm), on the other hand, is allowed to assign zero length to some non-zero vectors.

Chapter 3. Vector Spaces 19

A simple example is the 2-dimensional Euclidean space R^2 equipped with the Euclidean _____.

   a. Quasinorm
   b. -equivalence
   c. -module
   d. Norm

9. In geometry and trigonometry, an _____ is the figure formed by two rays sharing a common endpoint, called the vertex of the _____ . The magnitude of the _____ is the 'amount of rotation' that separates the two rays, and can be measured by considering the length of circular arc swept out when one ray is rotated about the vertex to coincide with the other Where there is no possibility of confusion, the term '_____' is used interchangeably for both the geometric configuration itself and for its angular magnitude (which is simply a numerical quantity.)
   a. ADE classification
   b. Abelian P-root group
   c. AKS primality test
   d. Angle

10. In mathematics, the _____ is an operation which takes two vectors over the real numbers R and returns a real-valued scalar quantity. It is the standard inner product of the orthonormal Euclidean space. It contrasts with the cross product which produces a vector result.
   a. Coefficient matrix
   b. Centrosymmetric matrix
   c. Complex structure
   d. Dot product

11. In geometry, two lines or planes (or a line and a plane), are considered _____ to each other if they form congruent adjacent angles (an L-shape.) The term may be used as a noun or adjective. Thus, referring to Figure 1, the line AB is the _____ to CD through the point B. Note that by definition, a line is infinitely long, and strictly speaking AB and CD in this example represent line segments of two infinitely long lines.
   a. -module
   b. Perpendicular
   c. 2-bridge knot
   d. -equivalence

12. In mathematics, a _____ in a (unital) ring R is an invertible element of R, i.e. an element u such that there is a v in R with

Chapter 3. Vector Spaces

uv = vu = 1_R, where 1_R is the multiplicative identity element.

That is, u is an invertible element of the multiplicative monoid of R. If $0 \neq 1$ in the ring, then 0 is not a _____.

Unfortunately, the term _____ is also used to refer to the identity element 1_R of the ring, in expressions like ring with a _____ or _____ ring, and also e.g. '_____' matrix.

   a. Ore condition
   b. Unit
   c. Ore extension
   d. Ascending chain condition on principal ideals

13. In linear algebra and functional analysis, a _____ is a linear transformation P from a vector space to itself such that $P^2 = P$. It leaves its image unchanged. Though abstract, this definition of '_____' formalizes and generalizes the idea of graphical _____.
   a. Projection
   b. Lumer-Phillips theorem
   c. C_0-semigroup
   d. Convolution power

14. In its simplest meaning in mathematics and logic, an _____ is an action or procedure which produces a new value from one or more input values. There are two common types of _____s: unary and binary. Unary _____s involve only one value, such as negation and trigonometric functions.
   a. ADE classification
   b. Abelian P-root group
   c. AKS primality test
   d. Operation

15. In the various branches of mathematics that fall under the heading of abstract algebra, the _____ of a homomorphism measures the degree to which the homomorphism fails to be injective. An important special case is the _____ of a matrix, also called the null space.

The definition of _____ takes various forms in various contexts.

a. Kernel
b. K-theory
c. Monomial basis
d. Completing the square

16. In mathematics, the _____ for a Euclidean space consists of one unit vector pointing in the direction of each axis of the Cartesian coordinate system. For example, the _____ for the Euclidean plane are the vectors

$$\mathbf{e}_x = (1,0), \quad \mathbf{e}_y = (0,1),$$

and the _____ for three-dimensional space are the vectors

$$\mathbf{e}_x = (1,0,0), \quad \mathbf{e}_y = (0,1,0), \quad \mathbf{e}_z = (0,0,1).$$

Here the vector e_x points in the x direction, the vector e_y points in the y direction, and the vector e_z points in the z direction. There are several common notations for these vectors, including $\{e_x, e_y, e_z\}$, $\{e_1, e_2, e_3\}$, $\{i, j, k\}$, and $\{x, y, z\}$.

a. -module
b. 2-bridge knot
c. -equivalence
d. Standard basis

17. In mathematics, the _____ of a vector space V is the cardinality (i.e. the number of vectors) of a basis of V. It is sometimes called Hamel _____ or algebraic _____ to distinguish it from other types of _____. All bases of a vector space have equal cardinality and so the _____ of a vector space is uniquely defined. The _____ of the vector space V over the field F can be written as $\dim_F(V)$ or as [V : F], read '_____ of V over F'.

a. Dual basis
b. Cofactor
c. Partial trace
d. Dimension

18. In linear algebra, a _____ or column matrix is an m × 1 matrix, i.e. a matrix consisting of a single column of m elements.

$$\mathbf{x} = \begin{bmatrix} x_1 \\ x_2 \\ \vdots \\ x_m \end{bmatrix}$$

The transpose of a _____ is a row vector and vice versa.

The set of all _____s forms a vector space which is the dual space to the set of all row vectors.

a. Normal basis
b. Column vector
c. Symplectic vector space
d. K-frame

19. In linear algebra, a _____ or row matrix is a 1 × n matrix, that is, a matrix consisting of a single row:

$$\mathbf{x} = \begin{bmatrix} x_1 & x_2 & \ldots & x_m \end{bmatrix}.$$

The transpose of a _____ is a column vector:

$$\begin{bmatrix} x_1 \\ x_2 \\ \vdots \\ x_m \end{bmatrix} = \begin{bmatrix} x_1 & x_2 & \ldots & x_m \end{bmatrix}^{\mathrm{T}}.$$

The set of all _____s forms a vector space which is the dual space to the set of all column vectors.

_____s are sometimes written using the following non-standard notation:

$$\mathbf{x} = \begin{bmatrix} x_1, x_2, \ldots, x_m \end{bmatrix}.$$

- Matrix multiplication involves the action of multiplying each _____ of one matrix by each column vector of another matrix.

- The dot product of two vectors a and b is equivalent to multiplying the _____ representation of a by the column vector representation of b:

$$\mathbf{a} \cdot \mathbf{b} = \begin{bmatrix} a_1 & a_2 & a_3 \end{bmatrix} \begin{bmatrix} b_1 \\ b_2 \\ b_3 \end{bmatrix}.$$

a. Dual spaces
b. Polynomial basis
c. Dual number
d. Row vector

20. In linear algebra, the _____ of a matrix is the set of all possible linear combinations of its column vectors. The _____ of an m × n matrix is a subspace of m-dimensional Euclidean space. The dimension of the _____ is called the rank of the matrix.
   a. Linear inequality
   b. Pseudovector
   c. Delta operator
   d. Column space

21. The _____ of an m-by-n matrix with real entries is the subspace of R^n generated by the row vectors of the matrix. Its dimension is equal to the rank of the matrix and is at most min(m,n.)

The column space of an m-by-n matrix with real entries is the subspace of R^m generated by the column vectors of the matrix.

Chapter 3. Vector Spaces

   a. Goodman-Nguyen-van Fraassen algebra
   b. Restriction of scalars
   c. Row space
   d. Differential graded algebra

22. The column _____ of a matrix A is the maximal number of linearly independent columns of A. Likewise, the row _____ is the maximal number of linearly independent rows of A.

Since the column _____ and the row _____ are always equal, they are simply called the _____ of A. More abstractly, it is the dimension of the image of A. For the proofs, see, e.g., Murase (1960), Andrea ' Wong (1960), Williams ' Cater (1968), Mackiw (1995).) It is commonly denoted by either rk(A) or _____ A.

   a. Schur complement
   b. Split-complex number
   c. Generalized Pauli matrices
   d. Rank

23. Let S be a set with a binary operation * . If e is an identity element of (S, *) and a * b = e, then a is called a _____ of b and b is called a right inverse of a. If an element x is both a _____ and a right inverse of y, then x is called a two-sided inverse, or simply an inverse, of y.
   a. -equivalence
   b. 2-bridge knot
   c. Left inverse
   d. -module

24. The _____ are natural numbers including 0 ' href='/wiki/0_(number)'>0, 1, 2, 3, ...) and their negatives (0, −1, −2, −3, ...). They are numbers that can be written without a fractional or decimal component, and fall within the set {...
   a. ADE classification
   b. Abelian P-root group
   c. AKS primality test
   d. Integers

Chapter 4. Linear Transformations, Orthogonal Projections, and Least Squares 25

1. In mathematics, especially in the area of abstract algebra known as ring theory, a _____ is a ring with 0 ≠ 1 such that ab = 0 implies that either a = 0 or b = 0 (the zero-product property.) That is, it is a nontrivial ring without left or right zero divisors. A commutative _____ is called an integral _____.
    a. Partially-ordered ring
    b. Coherent ring
    c. Subring
    d. Domain

2. In mathematics, a _____ is a function between two vector spaces that preserves the operations of vector addition and scalar multiplication. The expression 'linear operator' is in especially common use, for _____s from a vector space to itself In advanced mathematics, the definition of linear function coincides with the definition of _____.
    a. Real matrices
    b. Homomorphic secret sharing
    c. Linear map
    d. Rotation

3. In mathematics, an _____ is a vector space with the additional structure of inner product. This additional structure associates each pair of vectors in the space with a scalar quantity known as the inner product of the vectors. Inner products allow the rigorous introduction of intuitive geometrical notions such as the length of a vector or the angle between two vectors.
    a. ADE classification
    b. Abelian P-root group
    c. AKS primality test
    d. Inner product space

4. In linear algebra, functional analysis and related areas of mathematics, a _____ is a function that assigns a strictly positive length or size to all vectors in a vector space, other than the zero vector. A seminorm (or pseudonorm), on the other hand, is allowed to assign zero length to some non-zero vectors.

    A simple example is the 2-dimensional Euclidean space R^2 equipped with the Euclidean _____.

    a. Quasinorm
    b. -module
    c. -equivalence
    d. Norm

Chapter 4. Linear Transformations, Orthogonal Projections, and Least Squares

5. In mathematics, an _____ is a statement about the relative size or order of two objects, or about whether they are the same or not

- The notation a < b means that a is less than b.
- The notation a > b means that a is greater than b.
- The notation a ≠ b means that a is not equal to b, but does not say that one is bigger than the other or even that they can be compared in size.

In all these cases, a is not equal to b, hence, '_____'.

These relations are known as strict _____

- The notation a ≤ b means that a is less than or equal to b (or, equivalently, not greater than b);
- The notation a ≥ b means that a is greater than or equal to b (or, equivalently, not smaller than b);

An additional use of the notation is to show that one quantity is much greater than another, normally by several orders of magnitude.

- The notation a ≪ b means that a is much less than b.
- The notation a ≫ b means that a is much greater than b.

If the sense of the _____ is the same for all values of the variables for which its members are defined, then the _____ is called an 'absolute' or 'unconditional' _____. If the sense of an _____ holds only for certain values of the variables involved, but is reversed or destroyed for other values of the variables, it is called a conditional _____.

One can apply the same algebraic operations to inequalities as one would apply for solving equalities. For example, to find x for the _____ 10x > 20 one would divide 20 by 10 to obtain x > 2.

a. ADE classification
b. AKS primality test
c. Inequality
d. Abelian P-root group

6. A _____ is one of the basic shapes of geometry: a polygon with three corners or vertices and three sides or edges which are line segments. A _____ with vertices A, B, and C is denoted ABC.

In Euclidean geometry any three non-collinear points determine a unique _____ and a unique plane (i.e. a two-dimensional Euclidean space.)

Chapter 4. Linear Transformations, Orthogonal Projections, and Least Squares

   a. -module
   b. 2-bridge knot
   c. -equivalence
   d. Triangle

7. In mathematics, the _____ states that for any triangle, the length of a given side must be less than the sum of the other two sides but greater than the difference between the two sides.

In Euclidean geometry and some other geometries this is a theorem. In the Euclidean case, in both the less than or equal to and greater than or equal to statements, equality occurs only if the triangle has a 180° angle and two 0° angles, as shown in the bottom example in the image to the right.

   a. 2-bridge knot
   b. -module
   c. -equivalence
   d. Triangle inequality

8. In geometry, two lines or planes (or a line and a plane), are considered _____ to each other if they form congruent adjacent angles (an L-shape.) The term may be used as a noun or adjective. Thus, referring to Figure 1, the line AB is the _____ to CD through the point B. Note that by definition, a line is infinitely long, and strictly speaking AB and CD in this example represent line segments of two infinitely long lines.
   a. -equivalence
   b. -module
   c. 2-bridge knot
   d. Perpendicular

9. In linear algebra and functional analysis, a _____ is a linear transformation P from a vector space to itself such that $P^2 = P$. It leaves its image unchanged. Though abstract, this definition of '_____' formalizes and generalizes the idea of graphical _____.
   a. Projection
   b. C_0-semigroup
   c. Convolution power
   d. Lumer-Phillips theorem

10. In mathematics, two vectors are _____ if they are perpendicular, i.e., they form a right angle. The word comes from the Greek á½€ρθïŒς , meaning 'straight', and γωνῖα (gonia), meaning 'angle'. For example, a subway and the street above, although they do not physically intersect, are _____ if they cross at a right angle.

Chapter 4. Linear Transformations, Orthogonal Projections, and Least Squares

a. Orthogonal
b. Expression
c. Unital
d. Embedding

11. In linear algebra, a _____ is a set of vectors that, in a linear combination, can represent every vector in a given vector space or free module, and such that no element of the set can be represented as a linear combination of the others. In other words, a _____ is a linearly independent spanning set.
   a. Basis
   b. Chirality
   c. Minor
   d. Supergroup

12. In linear algebra, two vectors in an inner product space are _____ if they are orthogonal and both of unit length. A set of vectors form an _____ set if all vectors in the set are mutually orthogonal and all of unit length. An _____ set which forms a basis is called an _____ basis.
   a. Invertible matrix
   b. Overdetermined
   c. Elementary matrix
   d. Orthonormal

13. In mathematics, an _____ of an inner product space V (i.e., a vector space with an inner product), is a set of mutually orthogonal vectors of magnitude 1 (unit vectors) that span the space when infinite linear combinations are allowed. (In some contexts, especially in linear algebra, the concept of basis (linear algebra) means a set of vectors that span a space when only finite linear combinations are allowed.) Such an infinite linear combination is an infinite series, and the concept of convergence relied upon is defined in terms of the space's inner product.
   a. Eigendecomposition
   b. Orientation
   c. Overdetermined
   d. Orthonormal Basis

14. In mathematics, a _____ is a rectangular array of numbers. This way, matrices can record data that depend on multiple parameters. In particular they are used to keep track of the coefficients of multiple linear equations. Matrices are closely connected to linear transformations, which are higher-dimensional analogs of linear functions, i.e., functions of the form f(x) = c Â· x, where c is a constant. This map corresponds to a _____ with one row and column, with entry c. In addition to a number of elementary, entrywise operations such as _____ addition a key notion is _____ multiplication, which displays a number of features not encountered in numbers; for example, products of matrices depend on the order of the factors, unlike products of real numbers, say, where c Â· d = d Â· c for any two numbers c and d.

Chapter 4. Linear Transformations, Orthogonal Projections, and Least Squares

a. Matrix
b. Heap
c. Commutativity
d. Polynomial expression

15. In linear algebra, a _____ of a matrix is a decomposition of the matrix into an orthogonal and a right triangular matrix. _____ is often used to solve the linear least squares problem, and is the basis for a particular eigenvalue algorithm, the QR algorithm.

A _____ of a real square matrix A is a decomposition of A as

$$A = QR,$$

where Q is an orthogonal matrix and R is an upper triangular matrix

a. -equivalence
b. QR decomposition
c. LU decomposition
d. Crout matrix decomposition

16. In linear algebra, a _____ is a linear transformation that squares to the identity (R^2 = I, where R is in K dimensional space), also known as an involution in the general linear group. In addition to _____s across hyperplanes, the class of general _____s includes point _____s, reflections across subspaces of intermediate dimension, and non-orthogonal _____s.

A _____ over a hyperplane in an inner product space is necessarily symmetric, but a general _____ need not be as the example $\begin{bmatrix} 1 & 0 \\ 1 & -1 \end{bmatrix}$ shows.

a. Shear mappings
b. Morphism
c. Homomorphic secret sharing
d. Reflection

17. In its simplest meaning in mathematics and logic, an _____ is an action or procedure which produces a new value from one or more input values. There are two common types of _____s: unary and binary. Unary _____s involve only one value, such as negation and trigonometric functions.

Chapter 4. Linear Transformations, Orthogonal Projections, and Least Squares

a. Operation
b. Abelian P-root group
c. AKS primality test
d. ADE classification

18. In linear algebra, two n-by-n matrices A and B are called _____ if

$$B = P^{-1}AP$$

for some invertible n-by-n matrix P. _____ matrices represent the same linear transformation under two different bases, with P being the change of basis matrix.

The matrix P is sometimes called a similarity transformation. In the context of matrix groups, similarity is sometimes referred to as conjugacy, with _____ matrices being conjugate.

a. Cartan matrix
b. Skew-symmetric
c. Zero matrix
d. Similar

Chapter 5. Eigenvectors and Eigenvalues

1. In linear algebra, the _____ describes a particular construction that is useful for calculating both the determinant and inverse of square matrices. Specifically the _____ of the (i, j) entry of a matrix, also known as the (i, j) _____ of that matrix, is the signed minor of that entry.

Finding the minors of a matrix A is a multi-step process:

1. Choose an entry a_{ij} from the matrix.
2. Cross out the entries that lie in the corresponding row i and column j.
3. Rewrite the matrix without the marked entries.
4. Obtain the determinant M_{ij} of this new matrix.

M_{ij} is termed the minor for entry a_{ij}.

If i + j is an even number, the _____ C_{ij} of a_{ij} coincides with its minor:

$$C_{ij} = M_{ij}.$$

Otherwise, it is equal to the additive inverse of its minor:

$$C_{ij} = -M_{ij}.$$

If A is a square matrix, then the minor of its entry a_{ij}, also known as the i,j, or (i,j), or (i,j)[th] minor of A, is denoted by M_{ij} and is defined to be the determinant of the submatrix obtained by removing from A its i-th row and j-th column.

a. Complex structure
b. Resolvent set
c. Cofactor
d. Coefficient matrix

2. In mathematics, an _____ of a product of sums expresses it as a sum of products by using the fact that multiplication distributes over addition. _____s of polynomials are obtained by multiplying together their factors, which results in a sum of terms with variables raised to different degrees.

To multiply two factors, each term of the first factor must be multiplied by each term of the other factor.

Chapter 5. Eigenvectors and Eigenvalues

    a. Analytic subgroup
    b. Ordered vector space
    c. Equipotential surfaces
    d. Expansion

3. In linear algebra, a _____ of a matrix A is the determinant of some smaller square matrix, cut down from A by removing one or more of its rows or columns. _____s obtained by removing just one row and one column from square matrices (first _____s) are required for calculating matrix cofactors, which in turn are useful for computing both the determinant and inverse of square matrices.

    a. Supergroup
    b. Rng
    c. Purification
    d. Minor

4. In mathematics, the _____ of a ring R, often denoted char(R), is defined to be the smallest number of times one must add the ring's multiplicative identity element (1) to itself to get the additive identity element (0); the ring is said to have _____ zero if this repeated sum never reaches the additive identity. That is, char(R) is the smallest positive number n such that

$$\underbrace{1 + \cdots + 1}_{n \text{ summands}} = 0$$

if such a number n exists, and 0 otherwise. The _____ may also be taken to be the exponent of the ring's additive group, that is, the smallest positive n such that

$$\underbrace{a + \cdots + a}_{n \text{ summands}} = 0$$

for every element a of the ring (again, if n exists; otherwise zero.)

    a. Hereditary
    b. Characteristic
    c. Coherent ring
    d. Free ideal ring

5. In discrete mathematics, the _____ is used when solving recurrence problems. One can specify a recurrence relation of the form

$$t_n = At_{n-1} + Bt_{n-2}$$

where the value of t_n is dependent on the values of t_{n-1} and t_{n-2}. When solving a recurrence relation, the goal is to eliminate this dependency and derive an equation of the form

$$t_n = c_1 r_1^{\,n} + c_2 r_2^{\,n},$$

where c_1 and c_2 are constants and r_1 and r_2 are the roots of the _____

$$r^2 - Ar - B = 0,$$

where A and B are the constants defined in the original recurrence relation.

    a. -module
    b. 2-bridge knot
    c. -equivalence
    d. Characteristic equation

6. For each eigenvector of a linear transformation, there is a corresponding scalar value called an _____ for that vector, which determines the amount the eigenvector is scaled under the linear transformation. For example, an _____ of +2 means that the eigenvector is doubled in length and points in the same direction. An _____ of +1 means that the eigenvector is unchanged, while an _____ of −1 means that the eigenvector is reversed in sense.
    a. ADE classification
    b. Abelian P-root group
    c. AKS primality test
    d. Eigenvalue

7. For each _____ of a linear transformation, there is a corresponding scalar value called an eigenvalue for that vector, which determines the amount the _____ is scaled under the linear transformation. For example, an eigenvalue of +2 means that the _____ is doubled in length and points in the same direction. An eigenvalue of +1 means that the _____ is unchanged, while an eigenvalue of −1 means that the _____ is reversed in sense.
    a. Abelian P-root group
    b. ADE classification
    c. AKS primality test
    d. Eigenvector

Chapter 5. Eigenvectors and Eigenvalues

8. In mathematics, a _____ of a number x is any number which, when repeatedly multiplied by itself, eventually yields x:

$$r \times r \times \cdots \times r = x.$$

In terms of exponentiation, r is a _____ of x if

$$r^n = x$$

for some positive integer n. For example, 2 is a _____ of 16 since $2^4 = 2 \times 2 \times 2 \times 2 = 16$.

The number n is called the degree of the _____.

- a. Root
- b. Difference of two squares
- c. Rationalisation
- d. Cubic function

9. In mathematics, the _____s are an extension of the real numbers obtained by adjoining an imaginary unit, denoted i, which satisfies:

$$i^2 = -1.$$

Every _____ can be written in the form a + bi, where a and b are real numbers called the real part and the imaginary part of the _____, respectively.

_____s are a field, and thus have addition, subtraction, multiplication, and division operations. These operations extend the corresponding operations on real numbers, although with a number of additional elegant and useful properties, e.g., negative real numbers can be obtained by squaring complex (imaginary) numbers.

- a. -module
- b. -equivalence
- c. 2-bridge knot
- d. Complex number

10. In linear algebra, the _____ of an n-by-n square matrix A is defined to be the sum of the elements on the main diagonal (the diagonal from the upper left to the lower right) of A, i.e.,

$$\operatorname{tr}(A) = a_{11} + a_{22} + \cdots + a_{nn} = \sum_{i=1}^{n} a_{ii}$$

where a_{ij} represents the entry on the ith row and jth column of A. Equivalently, the _____ of a matrix is the sum of its eigenvalues, making it an invariant with respect to a change of basis. This characterization can be used to define the _____ for a linear operator in general.

Note that the _____ is only defined for a square matrix (i.e. n×n.)

a. Trace
b. Defective matrix
c. Coefficient matrix
d. Dot product

11. In mathematics, a _____ is a rectangular array of numbers. This way, matrices can record data that depend on multiple parameters. In particular they are used to keep track of the coefficients of multiple linear equations. Matrices are closely connected to linear transformations, which are higher-dimensional analogs of linear functions, i.e., functions of the form f(x) = c Â· x, where c is a constant. This map corresponds to a _____ with one row and column, with entry c. In addition to a number of elementary, entrywise operations such as _____ addition a key notion is _____ multiplication, which displays a number of features not encountered in numbers; for example, products of matrices depend on the order of the factors, unlike products of real numbers, say, where c Â· d = d Â· c for any two numbers c and d.
    a. Commutativity
    b. Matrix
    c. Polynomial expression
    d. Heap

12. In mathematics, the _____ is an operation which takes two vectors over the real numbers R and returns a real-valued scalar quantity. It is the standard inner product of the orthonormal Euclidean space. It contrasts with the cross product which produces a vector result.
    a. Dot product
    b. Complex structure
    c. Coefficient matrix
    d. Centrosymmetric matrix

13. In abstract algebra, the _____ of a module is a measure of the module's 'size'. It is defined as the _____ of the longest ascending chain of submodules and is a generalization of the concept of dimension for vector spaces. The modules with finite _____ share many important properties with finite-dimensional vector spaces.

Chapter 5. Eigenvectors and Eigenvalues

  a. Supermodule
  b. Morita equivalence
  c. Finitely generated module
  d. Length

14. A _____ is a specific type of recurrence relation.

An example of a recurrence relation is the logistic map:

$$x_{n+1} = rx_n(1 - x_n)$$

Some simply defined recurrence relations can have very complex (chaotic) behaviours and are sometimes studied by physicists and mathematicians in a field of mathematics known as nonlinear analysis.

Solving a recurrence relation means obtaining a closed-form solution: a non-recursive function of n.

  a. -equivalence
  b. -module
  c. 2-bridge knot
  d. Difference equation

15. In mathematics, the _____ are the following sequence of numbers:

The first two _____ are 0 and 1, and each remaining number is the sum of the previous two:

Some sources omit the initial 0, instead beginning the sequence with two 1s.

In mathematical terms, the sequence F_n of _____ is defined by the recurrence relation

with seed values

a. 2-bridge knot
b. -equivalence
c. -module
d. Fibonacci numbers

16. In mathematics, a _____ is a homogeneous polynomial of degree two in a number of variables. For example,

$$4x^2 + 2xy - 3y^2$$

is a _____ in the variables x and y.

_____s are central objects in mathematics, occurring for instance in number theory, geometry (Riemannian metric), topology (intersection forms on homology), and Lie theory (the Killing form.)

a. Rank
b. Quadratic form
c. Partial trace
d. Homogeneous coordinates

17. In linear algebra, a _____ matrix is a matrix that is 'almost' a diagonal matrix. To be exact: a _____ matrix has nonzero elements only in the main diagonal, the first diagonal below this, and the first diagonal above the main diagonal.

For example, the following matrix is _____:

$$\begin{pmatrix} 1 & 4 & 0 & 0 \\ 3 & 4 & 1 & 0 \\ 0 & 2 & 3 & 4 \\ 0 & 0 & 1 & 3 \end{pmatrix}.$$

A determinant formed from a _____ matrix is known as a continuant.

Chapter 5. Eigenvectors and Eigenvalues

a. -equivalence
b. 2-bridge knot
c. -module
d. Tridiagonal

18. In numerical linear algebra, the _____ is an eigenvalue algorithm; that is, a procedure to calculate the eigenvalues and eigenvectors of a matrix. The QR transformation was developed in 1961 by John G.F. Francis (England) and by Vera N. Kublanovskaya (USSR), working independently. The basic idea is to perform a QR decomposition, writing the matrix as a product of an orthogonal matrix and an upper triangular matrix, multiply the factors in the other order, and iterate.
    a. QR algorithm
    b. -equivalence
    c. 2-bridge knot
    d. -module

19. In linear algebra, the _____ of the monic polynomial

$$p(t) = c_0 + c_1 t + \ldots + c_{n-1} t^{n-1} + t^n$$

is the square matrix defined as

$$C(p) = \begin{bmatrix} 0 & 0 & \ldots & 0 & -c_0 \\ 1 & 0 & \ldots & 0 & -c_1 \\ 0 & 1 & \ldots & 0 & -c_2 \\ \vdots & \vdots & \vdots & \vdots & \vdots \\ 0 & 0 & \ldots & 1 & -c_{n-1} \end{bmatrix}.$$

With this convention, and writing the basis as $v_1, \ldots, v_n$, one has $Cv_i = C^{i-1}v_1 = v_{i+1}$ (for i < n), and v_1 generates V as a K[C]-module: C cycles basis vectors.

Some authors use the transpose of this matrix, which (dually) cycles coordinates, and is more convenient for some purposes, like linear recursive relations.

The characteristic polynomial as well as the minimal polynomial of C(p) are equal to p; in this sense, the matrix C(p) is the 'companion' of the polynomial p.

a. Wilkinson matrices
b. Matrix representation
c. Companion matrix
d. Levinson recursion

Chapter 6. Further Directions

1. In mathematics, a _____ decomposes a periodic function or periodic signal into a sum of simple oscillating functions, namely sines and cosines. The study of _____ is a branch of Fourier analysis. _____ were introduced by Joseph Fourier (1768-1830) for the purpose of solving the heat equation in a metal plate.

    a. -module
    b. 2-bridge knot
    c. -equivalence
    d. Fourier series

2. These solutions for n = 0, 1, 2, ... (with the normalization $P_n(1) = 1$) form a polynomial sequence of orthogonal polynomials called the _____s. Each _____ $P_n(x)$ is an nth-degree polynomial.

    a. Jacobi polynomial
    b. -equivalence
    c. -module
    d. Legendre polynomial

3. In mathematics, a _____ or pseudoinverse of a matrix A is a matrix that has some properties of the inverse matrix of A but not necessarily all of them. The term 'the pseudoinverse' commonly means the Moore-Penrose pseudoinverse.

    The purpose of constructing a _____ is to obtain a matrix that can serve as the inverse in some sense for a wider class of matrices than invertible ones.

    a. Generalized inverse
    b. Pascal matrix
    c. Sylvester equation
    d. Redheffer matrix

4. In mathematics, a generalized inverse or _____ of a matrix A is a matrix that has some properties of the inverse matrix of A but not necessarily all of them. The term 'the _____' commonly means the Moore-Penrose _____.

    The purpose of constructing a generalized inverse is to obtain a matrix that can serve as the inverse in some sense for a wider class of matrices than invertible ones.

    a. 2-bridge knot
    b. Pseudoinverse
    c. -module
    d. -equivalence

5. In mathematics, in particular functional analysis, the _____, or s-numbers of a compact operator T acting on a Hilbert space are defined as the eigenvalues of the operator $\sqrt{T^*T}$ (where T* denotes the adjoint of T and the square root is taken in the operator sense.) The _____ are nonnegative real numbers, usually listed in decreasing order $s_1(T)$, $s_2(T)$, ...

   a. -equivalence
   b. -module
   c. Singular values
   d. 2-bridge knot

6. In mathematics, a matrix is said to be _____ if in every row of the matrix, the magnitude of the diagonal entry in that row is larger than or equal to the sum of the magnitudes of all the other (non-diagonal) entries in that row, and if in at least one row of the matrix, the magnitude of the diagonal entry in that row is strictly larger than the sum of the magnitudes of all the other (non-diagonal) entries in that row. More precisely, the matrix A is _____ if

$$|a_{ii}| \geq \sum_{j \neq i} |a_{ij}| \quad \text{for all } i, \quad |a_{ii}| > \sum_{j \neq i} |a_{ij}| \quad \text{for at least one } i,$$

<_____>

where a_{ij} denotes the entry in the ith row and jth column. If the strictly greater than equality is true for all rows (all values of i), then the matrix is called strictly _____.

   a. Triangular matrix
   b. Minimum degree algorithm
   c. Diagonally dominant
   d. Circulant matrix

7. In linear algebra, functional analysis and related areas of mathematics, a _____ is a function that assigns a strictly positive length or size to all vectors in a vector space, other than the zero vector. A seminorm (or pseudonorm), on the other hand, is allowed to assign zero length to some non-zero vectors.

A simple example is the 2-dimensional Euclidean space R^2 equipped with the Euclidean _____.

   a. -module
   b. -equivalence
   c. Quasinorm
   d. Norm

Chapter 6. Further Directions

8. In mathematics, a _____ is a rectangular array of numbers. This way, matrices can record data that depend on multiple parameters. In particular they are used to keep track of the coefficients of multiple linear equations. Matrices are closely connected to linear transformations, which are higher-dimensional analogs of linear functions, i.e., functions of the form f(x) = c Â· x, where c is a constant. This map corresponds to a _____ with one row and column, with entry c. In addition to a number of elementary, entrywise operations such as _____ addition a key notion is _____ multiplication, which displays a number of features not encountered in numbers; for example, products of matrices depend on the order of the factors, unlike products of real numbers, say, where c Â· d = d Â· c for any two numbers c and d.

   a. Polynomial expression
   b. Heap
   c. Commutativity
   d. Matrix

9. In mathematics, a _____ is a natural extension of the notion of a vector norm to matrices.

In what follows, K will denote the field of real or complex numbers. Consider the space $K^{m \times n}$ of all matrices with m rows and n columns with entries in K.

A _____ on $K^{m \times n}$ satisfies all the properties of vector norms.

   a. Quasinorm
   b. -module
   c. -equivalence
   d. Matrix Norm

10. In ring theory, a branch of abstract algebra, a _____ is a ring in which the multiplication operation is commutative. The study of _____s is called commutative algebra.

Some specific kinds of _____s are given with the following chain of class inclusions:

   - _____s ⊃ integral domains ⊃ unique factorization domains ⊃ principal ideal domains ⊃ Euclidean domains ⊃ fields

A ring is a set R equipped with two binary operations, i.e. operations that combine any two elements of the ring to a third. They are called addition and multiplication and commonly denoted by '+' and '·', e.g. a + b and a · b.

   a. Going up
   b. Nilradical
   c. Differential calculus over commutative algebras
   d. Commutative ring

Chapter 6. Further Directions

11. In abstract algebra, a _____ is an algebraic structure with notions of addition, subtraction, multiplication and division, satisfying certain axioms. The most commonly used _____s are the _____ of real numbers, the _____ of complex numbers, and the _____ of rational numbers, but there are also finite _____s, fields of functions, various algebraic number _____s, p-adic _____s, and so forth.

Any _____ may be used as the scalars for a vector space, which is the standard general context for linear algebra.

   a. Tensor product of fields
   b. Generic polynomial
   c. Separable
   d. Field

12. In mathematics, a _____ is a type of algebraic structure. There is some variation among mathematicians as to exactly what properties a _____ is required to have, as described in detail below. However, commonly a _____ is defined as a set together with two binary operations (usually called addition and multiplication), where each operation combines two elements to form a third element.
   a. -equivalence
   b. 2-bridge knot
   c. Ring
   d. -module

13. The _____ are natural numbers including 0 ' href='/wiki/0_(number)'>0, 1, 2, 3, ...) and their negatives (0, −1, −2, −3, ...). They are numbers that can be written without a fractional or decimal component, and fall within the set {...
   a. Abelian P-root group
   b. Integers
   c. ADE classification
   d. AKS primality test

ANSWER KEY

Chapter 1
1. d 2. a 3. d 4. a 5. d 6. b 7. b 8. a 9. d 10. b
11. c 12. d 13. d 14. c 15. d 16. d 17. d 18. d 19. d 20. c
21. a 22. d 23. a 24. d 25. b 26. c 27. d 28. d

Chapter 2
1. a 2. a 3. d 4. a 5. c

Chapter 3
1. c 2. b 3. b 4. d 5. d 6. a 7. d 8. d 9. d 10. d
11. b 12. b 13. a 14. d 15. a 16. d 17. d 18. b 19. d 20. d
21. c 22. d 23. c 24. d

Chapter 4
1. d 2. c 3. d 4. d 5. c 6. d 7. d 8. d 9. a 10. a
11. a 12. d 13. d 14. a 15. b 16. d 17. a 18. d

Chapter 5
1. c 2. d 3. d 4. b 5. d 6. d 7. d 8. a 9. d 10. a
11. b 12. a 13. d 14. d 15. d 16. b 17. d 18. a 19. c

Chapter 6
1. d 2. d 3. a 4. b 5. c 6. c 7. d 8. d 9. d 10. d
11. d 12. c 13. b

www.ingramcontent.com/pod-product-compliance
Lightning Source LLC
Chambersburg PA
CBHW081220230426
43666CB00015B/2819